D0860373

Williamsburg

An Artist's & Writer's Sketchbook

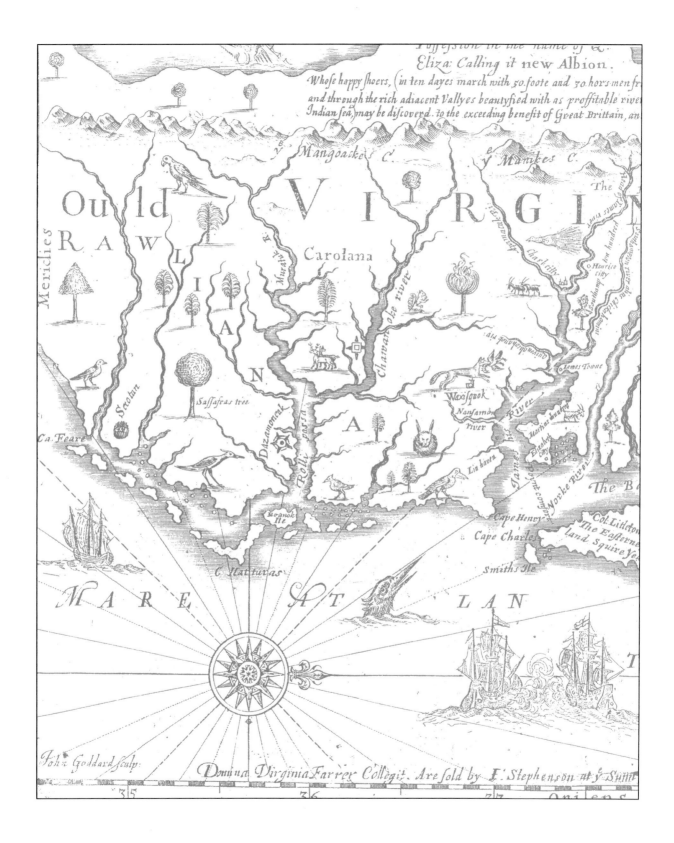

Poffeffion in the name of
Eliza: Calling it new Albion.

Whofe happy fhoers, (in ten dayes march with 50. foote and 30. hors men fr
and through the rich adiacent Vallyes beautyfied with as proffitable river
Indian fea, may be difcoverd. to the exceeding benefit of Great Brittain, an

Mangoacke's C.   y.e Mankes C.

Ou ld   V I R G I N   The

R A W L   Carolana

L   C. Henrico

I   city

A   Sassafras tree   Woosquok

N   Nansamond

Mericlies   River

Sroturn   James Towne

Ca. Feare   Roanok Ile

                              A

                    Roanok
                    Ile   Cape Henry
                                               Cape Charles   Col: Litleton
                                                               The Easterne
C. Hatturas   Smiths Ile   land Squire Ye

M A R E   A T   L A N

                                                                    T

John Goddard fculp: Domina Virginia Farrer Collegit. Are fold by I. Stephenson at y.e Sunn

        3.5   3.6   3.7   Oriens

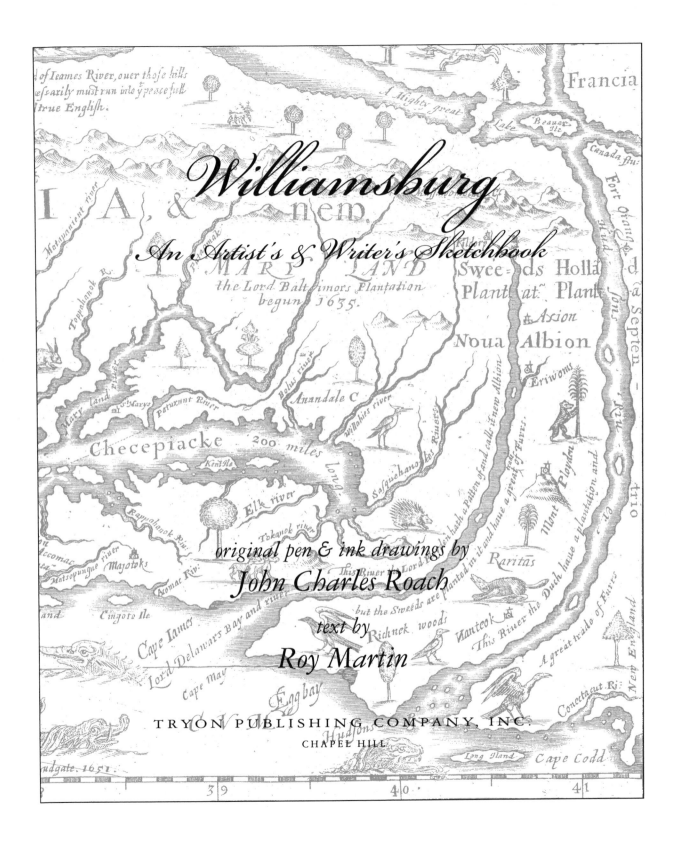

Williamsburg

An Artist's & Writer's Sketchbook

original pen & ink drawings by

John Charles Roach

text by

Roy Martin

TRYON PUBLISHING COMPANY, INC.

CHAPEL HILL

Dedication

For Sylvia and our children, Joseph R. Martin III, John Staton Martin,
Kathryn M. Allison, and Andrew G. Allison III.

— *Roy Martin*

Printed in the United States of America
Published by
Tryon Publishing Company, Inc.
P,O, Box 1138
Chapel Hill, North Carolina

Cover Design by John Roach and Julia Calhoun Williams
Book design by Julia Calhoun Williams & Maxine Mills

ISBN 1-884824-21-8

Table of Contents

Acknowledgements

The author would like to thank the following for their kindness and assistance in the preparation of the text for this book: Gayle Greve, Special Collections Librarian and Associate Curator, Rare Books and Manuscripts, at the Rockefeller Library in Colonial Williamsburg, Virginia; Diane Stallings, Jamestown Historian at the United States Park Service in Jamestown, Virginia; Margaret Cook, Manuscripts and Rare Books, Swem Library at the College of William & Mary in Williamsburg; the Reference Staff of the Newman Library at Virginia Polytechnic Institute & State University in Blacksburg, Virginia; the Reference Staff of the J.Y. Joyner Library at East Carolina University in Greenville, North Carolina; the Reference Staff of the University of Virginia Library in Charlottesville, Virginia; Anna Wentworth, Bob Allen and Tony Neuron at the Patrick Henry High School Library in Roanoke, Virginia; the Virginia Room at the Roanoke City Public Library in Roanoke, Virginia; and the City of Williamsburg.

Williamsburg

An Artist's & Writer's Sketchbook

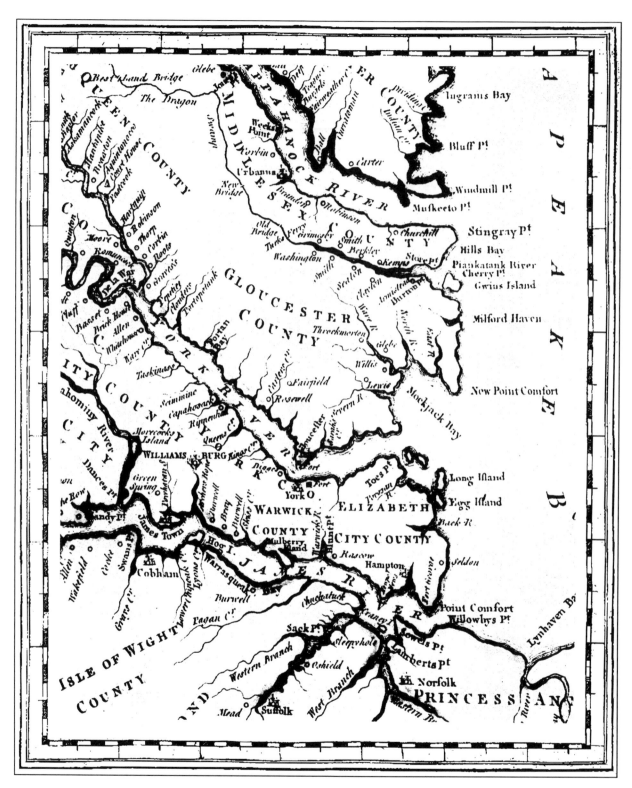

A portion of the Fry-Jefferson map of 1751.

Introduction

After establishing the first permanent English settlement in "Virginia" in 1607, the colonists at Jamestown suffered years of privation and sporatic conflict with the American natives they had, in effect, invaded. Ultimately, four elements contrived to bring about the search for a safer and more hospitable homesite.

The great Indian massacre of English settlers in 1622, Bacon's bloody rebellion of 1676, the 1693 founding of The College of William & Mary and swarms of mosquitos all planted seeds for Williamsburg.

The expansive high ground between the York and James Rivers, known as Middle Plantation, was not subject to the hoards of disease bearing insects that inhabited the low, swampy environment around the Jamestown settlement. Its topography also offered the best defense against hostiles. A Grand Assembly of the Council and Burgesses, meeting at Jamestown in 1633, ordered that a six-mile palisade be built across the peninsula to the east of the town, toward Old Point Comfort. This new fortification established Middle Plantation as a safety zone for people, property and livestock.

1676 brought young Nathaniel Bacon and his followers storming into Jamestown to protest Governor Sir William Berkeley's corrupt, desotic rule and his alleged ineptitude in dealing with marauding Native Americans. For years, Berkeley has dispensed favors, jobs, political positions and the best lands to his cronies. While his government grew wealthy from commerce and unreasonable taxes, the general populace suffered. This was not the English freedom they had been promised. By delaying elections, Berkeley kept his supporters in office; and by granting his followers titles to the majority of prime farmland, he forced settlers to venture farther afield and onto Indian hunting grounds in order to make their homes. The neighboring tribes, many faced with starvation, retaliated by attacking the isolated farmsteads. Berkeley responded with a confused and ineffectual policy that did nothing to protect them. Discontent boiled until a leader was found in the twenty-eight year old Bacon.

After Berkeley rebuffed his request for a commission to fight the increasing Indian incursions, Bacon took matters into his own hands. His troops raided native villages and he sent a steady stream of pleas to Jamestown seeking relief from Berkeley's oppressive regime. Addressing his men, Bacon alleged the Governor had created conflict simply because Bacon and his men were attempting to protect their "countrymen." There was nothing left to do, he said, but to go to Jamestown to deal with the treachery of Governor Berkeley and his followers. "...the [Berkeleyites] are all damned cowards and you shall see they will not dare to meete us in the field to try the justness of our cause and soe wee will [go] down to them," Bacon declared. And his rebels replied: "Amen, amen, wee are all ready and will rather die in the field than be hangeed like roges, or pereish in the woods, exposed to the favours of the mercyless Indians."

After months of rebellious attacks and counter-attacks, Bacon and his men swept into Jamestown, which Berkeley had deserted for safer ground in the East. They burned five of the Governor's homes, the Court House and other buildings in an effort to render the town useless if Berkeley should retake it.

Before his rebellion could succeed, Bacon died of dysentery. Without their fiery leader, his troops were finally defeated. Though the colony had survived its first civil conflict, the House of Burgesses considered the occupation of Jamestown as evidence that the locale was too vulnerable to future attack, from whatever quarter. Leading colonists were convinced that a new capital, on a more defensible site, was urgently needed.

Fears of marauding pirates also prompted citizens of York County to make the formal proposal in October, 1677. "And if a Towne be built for the Governor, Councill and Assembly to meet and for the General Court, we humbly propose the Middle Plantation as thought most fit, being the center of the country and also within Land most safe from foreign shipping, any place upon the River Side being liable to the Battery of their greatt Gunns."

The rising death toll from disease quickened the Virginia colony's drive toward a new capital city at Middle Plantation. Early in the life of the Jamestown colony, officials of the London Company, which had sponsored the settlement, instructed colonists not to build the town near the low marshes. However, in the minds of Jamestown settlers, the peninsula's clear defensive advantages outweighed the annoyance of flying insects. So, Jamestown was built, with little regard for the fertile mosquito breeding areas. Years of malaria and other illnesses followed. Somber processions to burial grounds became common, almost daily, events.

The London Company, beset by financial difficulties, lost its charter in 1624, the same year Virginia became a crown colony. But the company's impending demise did not forestall condemnation of its reckless disregard for the settlers' well-being. Fifteen years after Jamestown's founding, one critic wrote: "There havinge been as it is thought not fewer than tenn thousand soules transported thither ther are not through the aforenamed abuses and neglects above two thousand of them at the present to be found alive, many of them alsoe in a sickly and desperate estate. Soe that it may undoubtedly [be expected that unless the defects of administration be remedied] that in steed of a plantacion it will shortly gett the name of a slaughterhouse."

When Middle Plantation was proposed as the site for a new capital, the Jamestown colonists, exhausted from the agonies of illness and death, rejoiced. They may still be vulnurable to pirate raids, Indians and unfriendly European shipping, but a new city on high ground might at least save them from pestilence.

By April, 1699, a year after the rebuilt Jamestown State House burned again, establishing a new colonial capital had become a focus of the General Assembly but no final decision had been made. The Assembly convened at Jamestown on April 27 and quickly moved to Middle Plantation to escape the heat and insects. There, the session began routinely in meetings with Colonel Francis Nicholson, the new Royal Governor of Virginia. Four days later, the fate of the colonial capital had been determined.

By that time, the College of William and Mary had been built at Middle Plantation. The charter establishing The College, issued by the English king and queen in February, 1693, stated a founding purpose as the education of ministers to spread Christianity "among the Western Indians, to the glory of Almighty God, to make, found and establish a certain place of universal study, or perpetual College of divinity, philosophy, languages and other good arts and sciences..."

One student at the College, speaking to the House of Burgesses, noted progress already made toward a new town. "Here," he said of the proposed site near the college, "are great Helps and Advances already toward the

Beginning of a Town, a Church and Ordinary, several stores, two Mills, a Smiths Shop, a Grammar School and above all the college."

The General Assembly's path to abandoning the Jamestown capital for a Middle Plantation site led through five carefully-planned speeches by College of William and Mary students at a May Day celebration. Concentrating on educational values as well as the advantages of studying at a Virginia institution, the first two speakers tactfully laid groundwork for the third student. The young man spoke eloquently of the need for college and capital to be closely connected. "For in such a retired corner of the world," he said, "far from business, and action, if we make scholars, they are in danger of proving meer scholars, which make a very rediculous figure: made up of pedantry, disputaciousness, positiveness and a great many other ill qualities."

For worldliness and intellectual substance, should the colony relate education to business, commerce and government? The matter boiled down to common purpose, the speaker emphasized. The college needed the capital and the capital needed the college.

The final two speakers offered a brief history of the college and compliments to its patrons, asking that they encourage "...this accession of learning and ingenious arts..." so men everywhere might "acknowledge that the Colledge of William & Mary in Virginia is the mansion house of virtue, the Parnassus of the Muses and a seminary of excellent men."

The Assembly acted swiftly, deciding to erect public buildings "somewhere at Middle Plantation, nigh H.M. College of William and Mary." The new "citie" was to be called Williamsburg in honor of England's King William III. Having made their choice, the Burgesses set to work in 1700, carefully implementing a series of plans to launch Williamsburg as colonial Virginia's capital and to set patterns on which future development would rely.

A narrow trail, known as the Old Horse Path, nearly a mile long and running between the James and York rivers, was quickly widened to ninety-nine feet. The thoroughfare's new name, Duke of Gloucester Street, honored Queen Anne's son. A new Capitol building was erected on a site at the east end of Duke of Gloucester Street. At the far western end, almost a mile distant, stood The College of William & Mary's imposing Wren Building.

The building lots along the main street were restricted to a half-acre each. Other regulations dictated minimum size of houses as well as distance back from the street. An appointed board was to enforce these ordinances. Two ports, along navigable creeks, developed outside the village. Princess Anne's Port on Archer's Hope Creek provided access to the James River while Queen Mary's Port, along Queen's Creek, ran to the York.

Though the decision to move the seat of government from Jamestown to Williamsburg was firm, it should not be supposed that the total residency of Jamestown moved, "lock, stock, and barrel," in one great migration. Documentary and archeological evidence indicates that Jamestown continued as a town site well into the eighteenth century.

However, once the new settlement of Williamsburg was established, it rapidly grew and prospered. For eighty years, the ports bustled with tobacco and other commodities bound for foreign and domestic destinations. Carriages crowded the streets, some transporting affluent, well-dressed colonists to lavish balls at the Governor's Palace and to other social events. New homes and government buildings abounded. Young Colonel George Washington, fresh from French and Indian War skirmishes (1754-1763) on Virginia's terror-plagued frontier, came to town to talk strategy with Royal Governor Robert Dinwiddie and members of the Assembly. Thomas Jefferson occupied rooms at the Market Square Tavern while he studied law with

George Wythe. Virginia's first theatre as well as the first successful printing press and paper mill thrived in Williamsburg.

Writing in his book, PRESENT STATE OF VIRGINIA, published in London in 1724, the Reverend Hugh Jones, Professor of Natural Philosophy and Mathematics at the College of William & Mary, described the new capital city this way:

"Williamsburg is now incorporated (1722) and made a market town, and governed by a mayor and alderman; and is well stocked with rich stores, of all sorts of goods, and well furnished with the best provisions and liquors.

"Here dwell several very good families, and more reside here in their own houses at publick times.

"They live in the same neat manner, dress after the same modes, and behave themselves exactly as the gentry in London; most families of any note having a coach, chariot, berlin or chaise."

"The town is laid out regularly in lots or square portions, sufficient each for a house and garden; so that they don't build contiguous, whereby may be prevented the spreading danger of fire; and this also affords a free passage for the air which is very grateful in violent hot weather."

The Reverend Jones considered the Williamsburg building industry efficient, certainly in step with structural demands created by climate ranging from summer's sometimes blistering heat to hard winter storms.

"Here, as in other parts, they build with brick, but most commonly with timber lined with ceiling, and cased with feather-edged plank, painted with white lead and oil, covered with shingles of cedar, etc. tarred over at first; with a passage generally through the middle of the house for air-drought in summer.

"Thus their houses are lasting, dry, and warm in winter, and cool in summer, expecially if there be windows enough to draw air.

"Thus they dwell comfortably, genteely, pleasantly, and plentifully in this delightful, healthful, and (I hope) thriving city of Williamsburgh."

The city did thrive, as the Reverend Hugh Jones wished. But when revolutionary fever swept the American colonies and fighting began, Williamsburg became a notable and almost everlasting casualty.

By July 4, 1776, the British obsession with wrenching tax money from the colonies had resulted in incidents ranging from the deadly Boston Massacre (1770) to the Battles of Lexington and Concord (1775). Two days after these battles, Virginia's Royal Governor, Lord Dunmore, provoked armed rebellion when he seized gunpowder from the Williamsburg magazine and sent it to British warships in the nearby rivers. Brash, sharp-tongued Patrick Henry led a group of armed volunteers from Hanover County to demand the Governor return the powder or pay for it.

Lord Dunmore never returned the stores but paid the colony, dissolved the General Assembly and eventually fled, with his family, to the safety of a British ship. His departure signaled the end of British rule in Virginia. Governing power passed to the Assembly and then to the Virginia Convention of Delegates.

Meeting at the Capitol in Williamsburg in May, 1776, the Convention instructed Virginia's representatives to the Continental Congress in Philadelphia "to declare the United Colonies free and independent states." From that resolution evolved Jefferson's Declaration of Independence.

Two other critical resolutions resulted from that session: The Virginia Declaration of Rights which became the foundation of the U. S. Bill of Rights and The Virginia Constitution, which served as a model for the federal constitution. George Mason acted as chief architect of both measures.

Patrick Henry became the first governor of Virginia with Thomas

Jefferson succeeding him in 1779. In 1780, to escape the threat of British warships in the James and York Rivers, the General Assembly abruptly moved the capital to Richmond. Government, society, and their attendant commerce left Williamsburg. Thus, after eighty-one years, the fair "citie" lost its place in the mainstream of Virginia life.

Even with the convergence of British and then American and French forces on Williamsburg, the town benefitted little. The seige of Yorktown and the eventual surrender of Cornwallis brought an end to war but offered no opportunity for Williamsburg to regain its status. The capital remained in Richmond and the once vibrant city on the high ground between the James and York Rivers sank into isolation and decay.

"There's the Capitol, in which the fate of Empires has been decided like that of Ancient Rome," said Alexander Macaulay of Yorktown, passing through Williamsburg in 1783. "There the elegance of Demosthenes or Cicero, Mansfield or Camden has been far outshone..."

Another visitor, Ebenezer Denny of Pennsylvania, called the former capital "...a very handsome place but situate on even, pretty ground; streets and lots spacious—does not appear to be a place of much business—rather the residence of gentlemen of fortune."

But the wizard of lexicography, Noah Webster, visiting Williamsburg in 1785, best described some of the buildings and the college. "Decaying," he wrote. "...And so is the city by reason of the removal of the seat of Government to Richmond."

In THE AMERICAN UNIVERSAL GEOGRAPHY of 1793, writer Jedidiah Morse offered another sad profile: "Every Thing in Williamsburgh appears dull, forsaken and melancholy—no trade—no amusements but the infamous one of Gaming—no industry, and very little Appearance of religion." He described the Capitol and the area around it as "crumbling." At the time, the city could count about 1,400 residents.

Williamsburg's demise progressed, painfully.

During the period 1781-1859, fire destroyed treasured buildings, including the Governor's Palace, the Capitol, the main section of the College, and the Raleigh Tavern. Following a seventy-eight-year span of neglect and periodic disaster, the Civil War broke on Tidewater Virginia in 1862, when Union General George B. McClellan opened his Peninsula Campaign. McClellan pushed toward Richmond at the head of an army numbering more than 100,000 men. At Williamsburg, the Federals encountered Confederate General John Bankhead Magruder's force of defenders, which had dug into trenches, pits, redoubts and behind a network of barricades. On May 5, Confederate and Union soldiers clashed just east of the city in what became known as the Battle of Williamsburg. Wounded and dying streamed into the city. Some citizens opened their homes as field hospitals. Others strolled near the battlefield, risking themselves for a glimpse of the fighting.

At length, overall Rebel commander General James Longstreet withdrew toward Richmond, leaving Williamsburg under the control of Union forces.

Francois d'Orleans, French Royal Family observer with McLellan's troops, witnessed the Battle of Williamsburg. "The rains began to fall in torrents and poured down incessantly for thirty consecutive hours. The country became one vast lake, the roads were channels of liquid mud....The confederates had evacuated their works during the night. We soon entered them and watched the blue lines of federal infantry as they marched with banners flying into the town of Williamsburg to the sound of exploding magazines and caissons. Shortly after the General's [McClellan's] staff came in by a broad, fine street, bordered with acacias. All the shops were shut, but the inhabitants were for the most part to be seen in their doorways and windows, looking on us with a sombre, anxious air....From all the public buildings, churches, college and the like waved the yellow flag. They were crowded with the wounded left there by the enemy. At one end of the broad street, we debouched upon a handsome square, ornamented with a marble statue of Lord Botetourt, once governor of Virginia, and surrounded by the buildings of a celebrated college founded by the English government when Virginia was a pet colony. The wounded were lying upon the very steps of the college porticoes."

Except for one day, when Confederate troops briefly retook Williamsburg, the city remained under Union control until war's end. During the occupation, Federal soldiers set fire to the newly-reconstructed college and demolished other structures for bricks to build chimneys for officers' quarters.

After Appomatox and into reconstruction, the city's decline accelerated. Without slaves to tend gardens and lawns, to do household work and building repairs, and to provide labor for the ports, Williamsburg sank into what some observers at the beginning of the 20th Century described as near "rural slum" conditions.

It wasn't until 1917 that Williamsburg received a shot of new life. The United States entry into World War I brought a munitions manufacturing plant and more than 15,000 new residents. Property values swelled, generating revenue for improving streets and other public facilities. But after the war, the plant closed.

"Williamsburg on a summer day! The straggling street, ankle deep in dust, grateful only to the chickens, ruffling their feathers in perfect safety from any traffic danger," said Mayor George P. Coleman. "...The cows taking refuge from the heat of the sun, under the elms along the cidewalk. Our city fathers, assembled in friendly leisure, following the shade of the old Court

House around the clock, sipping cool drinks and discussing the glories of our past. Almost always our past!...The past alone held for them the brightness which tempted their thoughts to linger happily."

Williamsburg might have forever remained a sleepy rural town had it not attracted a brilliant cleric who had a passion for history. Dr. W. A. R. Goodwin, a native of Nelson County, Virginia, became rector of Bruton Parish Church in 1903, on the condition that the church interior be restored. That project completed, Dr. Goodwin left Williamsburg for a pastorate in New York. He returned in 1923, joining The College of William & Mary as head of the Department of Biblical Literature and Religious Education.

Inspired, doggedly determined, and persistent, he immediately launched his campaign of restoration and preservation.

"He'd come right up and catch you by the lapels and keep swaying from one foot to the other while he talked to you," one Williamsburg resident observed of Goodwin. "He was so convincing that I was certain that he could accomplish anything he might undertake."

Goodwin had heard of John D. Rockefeller's interest in historic sites and their preservation. In 1924 he met Rockefeller in New York. Goodwin's enthusiasm must have been impressive, for in 1926 Rockefeller visited Williamsburg. He was intrigued by Dr. Goodwin's vision, and after careful study of the detailed restoration plan, he quietly authorized purchase of the Ludwell-Paradise House on Duke of Gloucester Street for himself and his family.

Acquisitions continued—at a discreet but steady pace. Dr. Goodwin and Rockefeller agreed that widespread knowledge of land purchases could inflate property prices and endanger the project. As the process continued, Dr. Goodwin hired William Graves Perry, a partner in the Boston architectural firm of Perry, Shaw and Hepburn. Perry joined the restoration as an enthusi-astic specialist in colonial architecture and his mission was to plan and oversee the restoration. He arrived in 1927 and immediately set to work with Dr. Goodwin. Both continued the low-key approach, sometimes measuring parts of the city at night to avoid the eyes of curious citizens.

The extraordinary character of Williamsburg's resurrection can best be appreciated by understanding the context of the time during which the restoration began. There was literally no such thing as "colonial archeology" at the time; it was created and matured during the early days of research and exploration at the site.

According to Perry, architects weren't sure how to begin the task of restoration. He wrote: "There was little known precedent; there was no precedent in this country for a reconstruction or restoration of such scope and magnitude; there was no precedent for the reconstruction of a large group of buildings which were to represent the appearance of a complete town at a given period—and thereby hangs the tale of years of effort, conference and adjustment so to balance all considerations that the result, with its inevitable inconsistencies of coexistance and the like, would present a convincing and attractive appearance."

Furthermore, lack of experience became a factor. Perry believed finding a staff of architects, building craftsmen, draftsmen and mechanics to handle the painstaking work required would be nearly impossible.

"It was evident that investigation and training must precede restoration and that careful choice of associates and assistants must precede both. Young men from Virginia and elsewhere, already accomplished draftsmen, joined others already associated with the architects and an office was opened in old Bruton Church Parish House in 1927. "In a fertile soil of enthusiasm a beanstalk of data grew, so endowed with vigor that it seemed in its growth to refertilize itself. No house in Virginia was safe from invasion on Saturday afternoons, no owner or tenant secure from determined intrusion," Perry said.

News of the restoration spread. And by the time national news agencies got their stories of Williamsburg's impending revival, a simple—but popular —rhyme had surfaced in the old colonial capital.

"My gawd they've sold the town,
My gawd they've sold the town.
And it is said the news is spread
For many miles around.

They've sold the courthouse green,
I dare say all the people,
They'll sell the church, the vestry too
And even sell the steeple...

The streets will all come up
And the poles will all come down,
So take it from me stranger,
It's going to be some town."

Perry and his Boston partners, Thomas Mott Shaw and Andrew H. Hepburn, successfully organized a staff of draftsmen and researchers who drew plans for the early stages of restoration. They dug through mountains of documents including wills, diaries, bills of lading, inventory lists, and deeds as well has photographs, sketches and diagrams drawn for insurance policies. Archaeologists uncovered foundations of historic buildings such as the Governor's Palace and found assorted artifacts which gave the restoration direction toward the period authenticity that the project demanded. According to Shaw, the effort amounted to difficult, painstaking work but not without cheerfulness, enthusiasm and reward.

"The Virginia people were perfectly delightful about our visits. I can't say enough about the Virginia people—the way they were cordial and took us into their houses and told us everything they knew and they're so sympathetic," he wrote. "We had a few incidents, of course. Dear Miss Annie Galt down here, who owned one of the oldest houses in town on Francis Street, was a very distant connection of Mrs. Shaw's, by marriage. So shortly after I got down here, I thought it would be a nice thing to go around and say hello. I did and told her who I was. She was perfectly delightful. We had a nice chat and she said, 'Mr. Shaw, what are you doing down here.'

"I said, 'Well, I'm connected with this restoration.'

"She said, 'What! You mean to say Willie Goodwin has got you into this?'

"'Why yes,' I said. 'Don't you think it's interesting?'

"'Mr. Shaw,' she said, 'we think one Yankee invasion is enough.'

"So I took my leave very quickly after that."

By far, the most dramatic discovery leading to faithful reconstruction was that of the "Bodleian Plate," an engraving executed in 1740. This critical artifact, uncovered in the Bodleian Library at Oxford University in England, depicted the Wren Building, the Governor's Palace and the Capitol and shed new light on their design and construction. The vital architectural details revealed in the engraving were invaluable.

By 1935, work had largely been completed in the geographical area targeted for revitalization. That included blocks north and south of Duke of Gloucester Street and areas of the Capitol, Market Square and Palace Green.

More than four hundred buildings of post colonial era design had been demolished and eighteen moved out of the restored core. Of the colonial buildings, sixty-six had been restored. Another eighty-four had been rebuilt on period foundations.

According to the December, 1935 edition of RESTORATION OF WILLIAMSBURG: THE ARCHITECTURAL RECORD, issued by Perry, Shaw and Hepburn, Architects, "The Duke of Gloucester Street and its vicinity have resumed their colonial appearance, with lamp-posts, fences, brick walks, street surfaces, plantings and the like derived from authentic records."

Today, Williamsburg's 173-acre historic area is an active, thriving cultural center, dedicated to genuinely enlightening, as well as entertaining, representations of colonial life. Raleigh Tavern, the Magazine and Guardhouse and the Public Gaol are among the most popular attractions, along with The Governor's Palace and the Capitol. The addition of structures and themes relating to slave life in the town have added immeasurably to Williamsburg's historical authenticity. Wigmakers, silversmiths, blacksmiths, candlemakers and others demonstrate their crafts in shops lining Duke of Gloucester Street.

Williamsburg, Jamestown and Yorktown now form an "historic triangle," tracing American civilization from the beginning of the Virginia colony, through the Revolution, to present day. At Jamestown, a museum and architectural remnants of the first English settlement in the New World attract thousands of visitors each year. Powhatan Indian Village and recreated James Fort take imaginations back to the distant past, when venison roasted over open fires and children played in the dirt while colonists and Indians remained wary of one another.

Yorktown, several miles from Jamestown, celebrates the independence that came with the 1781 defeat of the British, under Lord Cornwallis, by

American and French forces. An extensive museum as well as the actual battlefield, complete with cannon, tell the story of the American Revolution's definitive moment.

But Williamsburg is the gleaming jewel, the hand-hewn symbol of creation and re-creation.

Wrote benefactor John D. Rockefeller Jr.: "The restoration of Williamsburg...offered an opportunity to restore a complete area entirely free from alien or inharmonious surroundings as well as to preserve the beauty and charm of the old buildings and gardens of the city and its historic significance. Thus it made a unique and irresistible appeal. As the work progressed, I have come to feel that perhaps an even greater value is the lesson that it teaches of the patriotism, high purpose and unselfish devotion of our forefathers to the common good."

Surveyor Theodorick Bland's 1699 sketch of early Williamsburg indicated 220 acres of land to be developed into the colonial capital. Early planners named Duke of Gloucester for the heir apparent to the English throne. The College of William and Mary stood at the western end of Duke of Gloucester Street and the Capitol was later built at the eastern end. Royal Governor Francis Nicholson took an active hand in planning the captial city, pushing through the assembly an ordinance requiring half-acre lotts. Houses built on Duke of Gloucester Street were to be exactly six feet back from the street and were to measure at least twenty feet by thirty feet. Eventually planners utilized a rectangular block scheme similar to layouts of Charleston and Philadelphia.

By the late 18th century Williamsburg had become a thriving center for trade, cultural activities and politics. Duke of Glocester Street served as one conduit for traffic to the ports near the James and York Rivers. Shops along the street displayed craftsmen's wares and the latest fashions and innovations from Europe. During "publick times," the capital's normal population of 3,000 swelled by another thousand or more who came in from the country-side. Patrons jammed inns and taverns such as the King's Arms and the Raleigh. Crowds were attracted to events ranging from fairs and cock fights to greased pig chases. The elite dined at the palace with the Royal Governor. London theater companies performed comedic spoofs of famous personages of the day as well as Shakespeare's tragedies.

B efore the Revolution, Williamsburg residents registered little surprise
when George Washington rode along Duke of Gloucester Street.
Washington, as Colonel of the Virginia Regiment during the French and
Indian War, frequently came to the capital to confer with Governor Robert
Dinwiddie on the best ways to protect settlers on the colony's savage frontier.
After a dispute with Dinwiddie over ranking of officers under his command,
Washington resigned from the colonial army. He later served in the House
of Burgesses and The Virginia Convention of Delegates. That meant
traveling to Williamsburg to meet with Patrick Henry, Thomas Jefferson,
George Wythe, George Mason and others to press the American colonies'
bid for independence. When Americans died at Lexington and Concord, he
was ready to fight. He refused pay, except for his expenses. "...as no pecuniary
consideration could have tempted me to accept this arduous employment at
the expense of my domestic ease and happiness, I do not wish to make any
profit from it." He took command of the Continental Army in July, 1775.

Patrick Henry came to the Virginia House of Burgesses in 1765, about the time Parliament passed the much-despised Stamp Act. At 29, Henry, a lawyer, had made his reputation as a fiery courtroom orator and a bitter opponent of what he considered the King's injustices against common people. When the Stamp Act became law, Virginia legislators, meeting at the Capitol in Williamsburg, voiced little opposition. But Patrick Henry rose and fearlessly offered resolutions contending Parliament had no right to tax the colonies. "Caesar had his Brutus; Charles the First, his Cromwell; and George the Third..." Cries of treason! treason! erupted in the chamber. Unruffled, he finished: "...and George the Third may profit by their example. If this be treason, make the most of it!" The resolutions passed.

Whether at the Governor's Palace or any other site in colonial Williamsburg, Thomas Jefferson drew a crowd. As a member of the House of Burgesses and later the Virginia Convention of Delegates, he quickly became part of the colony's inner circle of revolutionaries. He knew the city well. He graduated from William and Mary College in 1762 after studying moral philosophy, mathmatics and literature with Dr. William Small. Later, he studied law under George Wythe, one of the signers of the Declaration of Independence. His greatest service during the Revolution was as thinker, writer of the Declaration of Independence, and champion of individual freedom. Following the war, it was frequently said in Virginia: "Washington was the sword of the Rebellion, Patrick Henry its tongue and Jefferson its pen."

George Wythe, sometimes called Virginia's "forgotten patriot," traveled a varied route through the colonial capital to attend to his daily pursuits as lawyer, burgess, classical scholar, teacher and revolutionary statesman. A friend and pupil, William Munford, described Wythe as a middle-sized man. "His head was very round with a high forehead; well-arched eyebrows; prominent blue eyes, showing softness and intelligence combined; a large aquiline nose, rather small but well-defined mouth, and thin whiskers not lower than his ears...His face was kept smoothly shaven...His countenance was exceedingly benevolent and cheerful." Wythe counted Thomas Jefferson as his most gifted student and likely provided foundation for the spirit of individual liberty found in the Declaration of Independence and later in Jefferson's 1786 Virginia Statute of Religious Liberty. His home, located on the west side of Palace Green, was built around 1753 by Wythe's father-in-law, planter and architect Richard Talliaferro.

George Mason, author of the Virginia Declaration of Rights, got his first
tast of palaces, royal governors, and Williamsburg when he served one year
(1759-1760) in the House of Burgesses. After completing his term, Mason
decided he wanted no part of public service and returned to Gunston Hall, his
vast estate on the Northern Neck. But when revolution came, the scholarly
Mason found himself back in the capital and in the fight to banish English
control. In a spring 1776 meeting in Williamsburg, the Virginia Convention
of Delegates chose Mason to guide a committee in the drafting of a resolution
to push the Continental Congress to declare independence. In short order, the
committee presented a fourteen-point document, ten of the points authored
by Mason, focused squarely at the rights of men. He contended that men are
by nature free and have certain basic rights that cannot be tampered with,
including "the enjoyment of life and liberty, with the means of acquiring
and possessing property, and pursuing and obtaining happiness and safety."
The Virginia Declaration discussed three branches of government, arbitrary
suspension of laws, and the necessity of a free press. Mason's commitment
and personal labor gave Jefferson substance for the Declaration of Independence
and foundation for the Bill of Rights.

A session of the House of Burgesses was as much a social as a political event. Members came from small towns, from plantations and from backwoods settlements. For an aspiring burgess, dress spoke to origins and education, wealth and status, and even offered clues as to political potential. Planters had access to fine fabrics from England while homespun clothing marked a lawmaker from less sophisticated circumstances. Silk was a favorite material for suits which included coat, waistcoat and knee britches with hose. Shoes with gold or silver buckles were imported from England or made in the colony. A broad-brimmed hat, complete with plume, was a wardrobe necessity. Wearing a wig and powdered hair became the fashion rage in the late 16th century but declined after 1750.

Much of the critical, pre-revolutionary debate took place in Williamsburg's taverns. Jefferson, Washington, Wythe, Mason, Peyton Randolph, Patrick Henry and other leaders of the movement for independence gathered regularly for ale, dinner and lively conversation. The most popular hostelry was Raleigh Tavern, a square, wooden building on Duke of Gloucester Street, a half-block west of the Capitol. The establishment gained fame as the "second capitol of the colony" because legislators convened there on the two occasions when the assembly was dissolved by royal governors. Sessions at The Raleigh culminated in a call to the other colonies for the First Continental Congress. The Raleigh's motto, inscribed over the mantel in the Apollo Room read: "Hilaritas Sapientiae et Bonae Vitae Proles" or "Jollity, the offspring of wisdom and good living."

Cane and silk hats, some trimmed with French flowers, silk hoods, calash
bonnets as well as imported riding hats in bright greens, blues, and whites
could be purchased individually or by the cartload at the millinery shop on
Duke of Gloucester Street. Inside, a tasteful colonial woman could find
counters laden with frills and accessories, including colored plumes, cloaks
of flowered satin, ribbons, buttons, and fans. She could also purchase soaps,
knitting needles and other necessities. One 17th century shop advertised:
Bristol stone and pearl sleeve buttons, bags for wigs, Irish linens, silver shoe
buckles and "sundry other articles too tedious to mention."

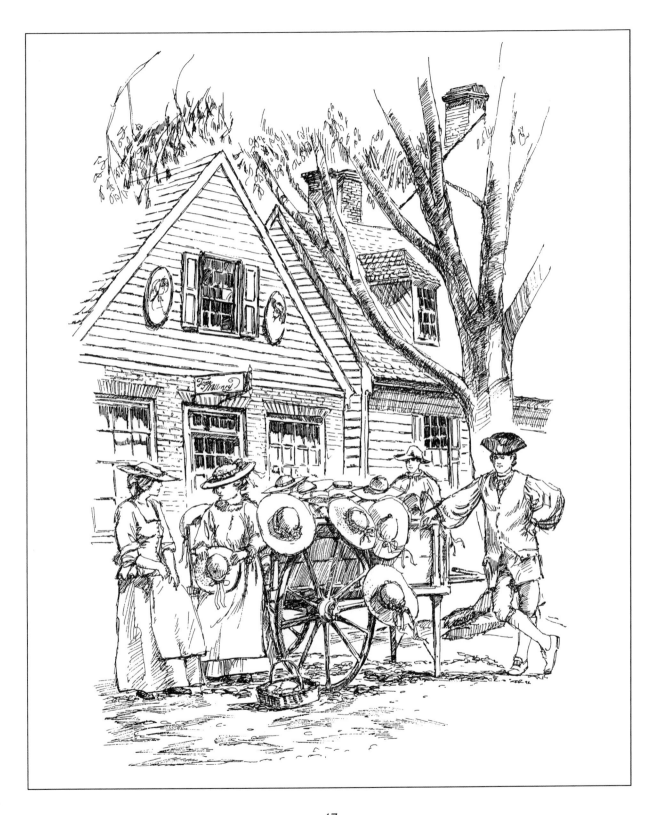

The occasion might have been a post-harvest festival at the elegant home of a planter, a House of Burgesses social or Easter Sunday at Bruton Parish Church. Williamsburg's social and religious life resulted in a flourishing of the craft of dressmaking during the town's reign as colonial capital. Women's fashions usually drew on English influences. Travelers returning from London brought word of new fashion sensations as well as the evidence itself—new wardrobes. Most dressmakers ordered materials from England, hoping to provide a satisfying combination of cloth and popular styling. Eighteenth century ladies of Williamsburg wore dresses of satin and velvet, broadcloth, and woolens. Prunella, a heavy fabric for petticoats, became popular as a material for women's shoes.

Englishman John Kello, writing to London from Hampton in 1755, noted the popularity of balls in Virginia and the colonial enthusiasm for dancing. "Dancing is the chief diversion here, and hunting and racing." Balls were frequently held in private homes, estates or at family or public gatherings. To the music of French horns, flutes and strings, dancers stepped lively to jigs or reels or country dances, later known as square dances. "Squire" Richard Lee of nearby Lee Hall, hosted a ball that lasted four days. More than seventy people attended and were reported to have been "quite wearied out for the experience." By far, the most popular dance in Colonial Virginia was the "Sir Roger de Coverley" or "Virginia Reel," a country dance which involved steps in marching cadence, and was traditionally the final dance of each ball.

The Royal Governor's House—called a "Palace" because of the public expense in building it—was frequently the scene of glittering evenings. Such occasions celebrated birthdays of British royalty or special holidays. The 1736 birthday of the Prince of Wales was marked by "...firing of guns, displaying of colors and other public demonstrations of joy, and at night his honor, the Governor, gave a ball, and an elegant entertainment to the ladies and gentlemen." On the night of the King's birthday in 1752, the festivities included a fireworks display in front of the palace and an appearance by "...the Emperor and Empress of the Cherokee Nation with their Son, the young Prince." Palace construction began about 1706 and was completed about 1720. The mansion, filled with elaborate furnishings and surrounded by gardens, served as home for seven royal governors as well as Patrick Henry and Thomas Jefferson, elected governors of Virginia.

Williamsburg was a haven for music lovers. Evening sessions of musical entertainment drew enthusiasts to private homes or to The College of William and Mary. Flute, violin, harpsicord or spinet were the most common instruments. During the years from the mid-eighteenth century to the Revolution, either a spinet or harpsicord could be found in nearly every home. Wealthy planters made certain that their daughters were taught to play, usually by a traveling music teacher. Music for guests and family featured popular love songs, performed by the young ladies, hymns, or dance tunes, which quickly set most gatherings high-stepping.

The choice for an evening's dining might have taken a colonial couple to Christiana Campbell's Tavern or the King's Arms, the Raleigh, Southall's or Josiah Chowning's. The atmosphere was enhanced by strolling musicians and the tasty table fare offered such delicacies as peanut soup, seafood chowders, game pie or Virginia Ham, a wide variety of native vegetables, the famous Sally Lunn bread and plum or fig ice cream. Tavern keepers were expected to carry an extensive and varied stock. In addition to fine ales, favorites of the day were Madeira and Fial as well as wines, including claret and port, from France and other European countries.

A large fireplace served as the centerpiece of the colonial kitchen. Constructed of brick, cooking fireplaces usually measured about twelve feet in width. The wood mantle offered hooks useful in hanging essential cooking tools such as ladles, skimmers and heavy spoons. Andirons on the fireplace floor supported a wood fire. Spits turned roasting meats. Utensils needed for full-scale food preparation included iron pots (some holding up to fifteen gallons), frying pans, brass kettles, mortar and pestle, a grater and a gridiron. Spices, flavorings, raisins and almonds came on the ships from England and could be bought at Williamsburg stores. Vegetables grew in home gardens. Peaches were almost always plentiful and could be found in the markets or the countryside. Meat, poultry and fish were readily available in shops. Cooking fires burned day and night. Kitchens were located a short distance away from the main house because of the fire hazard and to keep heat and undesirable odors away from the living quarters.

"I hereby acquaint the publick that I have opened a tavern...where all who please to favor me with their custom may depend upon the best of entertainment for themselves, servants and horses, and good pasturage." This notice, dated October 10, 1766, announced the opening of Chowning's Tavern. Essentially an alehouse, the Duke of Gloucester Street tavern didn't serve patrons as sophisticated as those who frequented Raleigh Tavern or Southall's. They came from outlying farms, ships at the river docks, shops along the street or from the court, where they might have had business or answered charges. Chowning's didn't fare well in the competitive world of Williamsburg taverns. It closed after two years of operation.

During the eighty years that Williamsburg served as colonial capital, the militia remained on alert—if not engaged with local Indians, the combined French and Indian forces, and later, British troops. In 1755, Virginia had an estimated population of 230,000 with 27,000 enrolled in the militia. Being a militiaman meant training and that meant drilling, cleaning and maintaining weapons, and seeing to uniforms, horses, supply and ammunition wagons. Williamsburg women took responsibility for feeding on-duty militia. In good weather, militiamen enjoyed meals on the lawn adjacent to the drill field and Powder Magazine.

The College of William and Mary was established at Middle Plantation in 1693. After Harvard, it became the second college in the British Colonies. English architect Sir Christopher Wren designed the principal campus structure which bears his name. Construction of foundations began in 1695, making it the oldest academic building in English America. In the college's early days, it housed teachers and students. Interior facilities included a kitchen, great hall and dining room. Beneath Wren Chapel, built in 1732, are buried colonial figures Lord Botetourt, Sir John Randolph, John Randolph, the "Tory," and Peyton Randolph, first President of the Continental Congress. Initially founded as a ministerial school, William and Mary evolved into an institution that attracted and nurtured three presidents, Jefferson, Monroe and Tyler; George Wythe, the first law professor in the United States; and U. S. Supreme Court Chief Justice John Marshall.

James Blair, Anglican minister and educator, founded the College of William and Mary. Blair served as the Lord Bishop of London's Commissary in Virginia. On February 8, 1693 he received the royal charter from King William and Queen Mary. The charter emphasized the training of ministers, the education of youth in letters and manners, and the proliferation of the Christian faith among the Indians. To build the campus, Blair prevailed upon the King and Queen for "2,000 pounds from quitrents, 20,000 acres, a penny tax on each pound of tobacco exported from Maryland and Virginia to the other English Colonies, and a share of the fees and profits of the office of Virginia's Surveyor General." The minister also persuaded pirates to contribute loot in exchange for lighter sentences or pardons. Blair became the first President of The College of William and Mary and served for fifty years.

Bruton Parish Church was first built at Middle Plantation in 1683. After the colonial capital was moved from Jamestown to Williamsburg, a second building was completed in 1715 to accommodate parishioners who moved, along with the government, to the new settlement. The tower was added in 1769. Designed by Royal Governor Alexander Spotswood, the church on Duke of Glouscester Street, has been in continuous use since the colonial era. It was once the seat of Anglican authority in Virginia. Bruton Parish routinely welcomed royal governors as well as members of the House of Burgesses to worship. Students from the College of William and Mary occupied a special reserved gallery. As young men, Presidents Washington, Jefferson, Monroe and Tyler attended the church.

Colonial courts dealt with a variety of offenses or civil disputes. A stern, robed and bewigged judge sat high above a defendant or petitioner to the court. Fines and judgements were ordered satisfied by cash or commodity, most often tobacco. Judges handled such matters as issuing peace bonds and dispatching court orders. They also approved road building, set tax rates, called elections and could terminate the license of an ill-behaved tavern owner. Judges also frequently inspected scales at the tobacco warehouse— just to insure fair-dealing.

The pillory offered offenders a quick and easy lesson in punishment. The wooden stocks grated skin from the neck and wrists and offered sensations of choking. The idea was to give a petty criminal warning that repeated offences could lead to a more severe fate—hanging. In more serious cases, criminals were housed in The Public Gaol or jail, built in 1701 near the Capitol. One of the most famous prisoners housed there was Henry Hamilton, known as the "hair-buyer," captured by George Rogers Clark at Vincennes, Indiana. Hamilton was charged with inciting Indians against the colony by paying bounties for colonists' scalps. Blackbeard's pirates languished in the Gaol prior to hanging. Prisoners were usually held together in a single room, confined by handcuffs and riveted leg irons.

The Powder Magazine served as the focal point of militia activity during the colonial period. Erected in 1715 to protect the colony's stores of military equipment, gunpowder, balls, mines and bombs, the Magazine was strengthened during the French and Indian War (1754-1763) by the addition of a surrounding wall and a guardhouse. In April, 1775, Governor Dunmore seized ammunition and powder from the Magazine and had it placed aboard a British ship lying offshore from the river ports. The action enraged colonists and prompted firebrand Patrick Henry to lead an armed group to Williamsburg to demand return of the stores—or payment for them. These actions were indicative of the Royal Governor's growing distrust of the colonists and their determination to move towards a separation from England. After the capital moved to Richmond, the building had many uses including a church, dancing school, Confederate arsenal, and livery.

Mustering colonial troops fell to the drummers, who thumped out the message calling volunteers from their work at forges, fields, lumber mills or cooper's shop. After British General Braddock's 1755 defeat by French and Indians forces in the Ohio River Valley, Virginia's Governor Dinwiddie requested the House of Burgesses "...make a law to strengthen the malitia by obliging every subject capable of bearing arms to be properly trained, disciplined and ready to serve his country when needed..." The Burgesses responded quickly by raising taxes to provide and maintain armed forces needed to protect the colony's western frontiers.

The thundering drums and shrill tones of a marching fife and drums corps never failed to stir colonial Virginians as it paraded down dusty Duke of Glouscester Street. The sounds meant celebration—of a victory over French and Indians or good news from the North during the Revolution. On other occasions—at fairs, horse races or ceremonial public events—the fife and drum corps, along with marching militia, performed, reminding colonists they must continue to support a strong military to combat the dangers lurking in the deep forests and distant mountains of the colony.

Volunteer colonial soldiers bore the burden of protecting settlers in the west, as well. Before the Revolution, the problem of recruiting volunteers seemed almost insurmountable. The Militia Act of August 1755 proved discriminatory against the poor. A man could be exempted from service if he hired a substitute or paid a fine. Frontiersmen refused to leave their families as long as the threats from allied French and Indians continued. Speaking to the General Assembly on October 27, 1755, Governor Dinwiddie asked for laws to strengthen the militia, to effect stronger army discipline, and to punish deserters. By May, 1756 modifications had been legislated for volunteer enlistment and conscription. The Reverend James Maury found lawmakers' efforts had achieved results. "It is very pleasing consideration to observe the general spirit and patriotism, and the resentment against the common enemy, which seems to have diffused itself through every rank of men," he wrote after visiting Washington and colonial volunteers in the field.

Two ports served nearby colonial Williamsburg. All manner of shipping sailed up Queen's Creek from the York River to Queen Mary's Port's Capital Landing. From the James, vessels used College Creek to reach Queen Anne's Port at its College Landing. Both ports were about a mile from the capital. Typical incoming cargoes consisted of rum, lemons, ivory, sugar and mahogany. Loads on departing ships included tobacco, flour, grain and other items of interest to English consumers.

Tobacco reigned as the colony's chief export. Planters transported their crops to primary shipping ports in large wooden casks called hogsheads. Ships often picked up their cargo at plantation wharves. This was the most inexpensive method of shipment. Transportation to primary ports such as Queen Mary's or Queen Anne's involved small boats— sloops or "tobacco boats." The tobacco boat was a double dugout canoe, fifty to sixty feet long and from four to five feet wide. The canoes were connected by crossbeams and pins, poled by a crew of two to three men, and could carry five to ten hogsheads. The "golden weed" held such an exalted place in the colonial economy that clergy, government officials, and soldiers were paid in tobacco. The colony exported a yearly average of 50,000 hogsheads of the precious leaf.

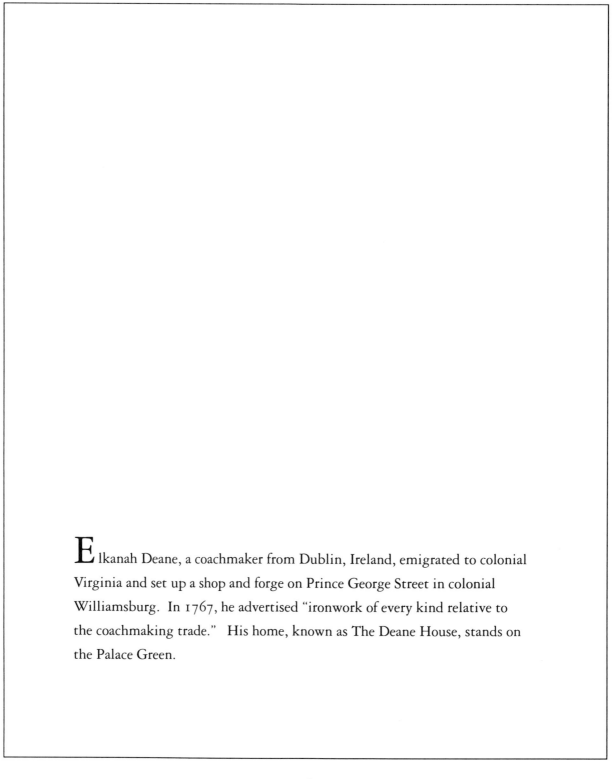

Elkanah Deane, a coachmaker from Dublin, Ireland, emigrated to colonial Virginia and set up a shop and forge on Prince George Street in colonial Williamsburg. In 1767, he advertised "ironwork of every kind relative to the coachmaking trade." His home, known as The Deane House, stands on the Palace Green.

From the affluent to the less-than-wealthy, the horse was the primary source for transportation. At the forge, the routine of shoeing horses involved examining hooves for general condition or damage, making the correct size iron shoes and nailing them into place. The forge also made harness and carriage buckles as well as metal decorations for coaches, which might include a purchaser's family coat of arms.

I nside the forge, sparks flew from clanging hammers and clouds of steam
rose from water buckets into which the smiths thrust red-hot pieces of metal,
part of the tempering process. The village blacksmith, whether alone or with
helpers, constituted a vital industry in any settlement. Every metal tool, piece
of hardware, cooking utensil, or implement of any kind was produced, and
perhaps later repaired, at the smithy's forge. In addition to items for horse and
carriage, the forge fashioned hinges, knives, sword guards, nails, pickaxes,
felling-axes, chisels, hatchets, drill bits and axle parts.

Making hogsheads, the large wooden casks for shipping tobacco, kept colonial Virginia coopers busy. Strength was the primary priority. To get their crop to market or to a port, planters often pegged shafts into the headings, hooked up a horse or ox and rolled the hogshead on its way. In 1724, Hugh Jones, writing in *The Present State of Virginia*, observed: "The tobacco is rolled down, drawn by horses, or carted to convenient Rolling Houses, whence it is conveyed on board the ships in flats or sloops." Shippers also used the cooper's products for transporting various cargoes, such as wine, sugar, or flour, by water or wagon.

Cutting timber and transforming it into lumber for building probably ranks as Virginia's first industry. Houses, furniture, boats, mantles and mantle facings, wheelbarrows, carts and wagons—all wood products were continuing necessities as Williamsburg grew. At the lumber mill, heavy logs were carried in to workers who manned crude saws and planers. Houses generally consisted of wood framing faced with weatherboarding. The popularity of wood in colonial house-building resulted from a common theory that brick walls often became damp. Jefferson wrote in 1784: "...private buildings are very rarely constructed of brick or stone; much the geater portion being of scantling and boards, plastered with lime."

As Williamsburg moved into the eighteenth century, the business of carpenters and masons burgeoned and they took lead roles in the development of the colonial capital. Not only did government and college buildings become numerous but free-standing houses also dotted the 220 acres comprising the original town plan. An early house ususally consisted of a story and a half. Wood shingles covered the steep, A-roof. A chimney stood at each end of the house. Later plans and additions included expanded interiors, allowing for more living space, hallways and parlors. Exteriors remained plain and unpretentious, excluding front columns, a feature on some of the more ornate homes built by large planters.

Colonists from agrarian roots in England understood the need for sturdy fencing. But in 1705, the Virginia General Assembly, in an effort to protect Williamsburg gardens from stray cattle and horses, took necessity a step further. Legislators passed a law requiring that the lots contiguous to Duke of Gloucester Street be fenced. Owners would "...inclose the said lots, or half acres, with a wall, pails, or post and rails, within six months after the building, which the law requires to be erected thereupon, shall be finished." The law required the fences be four and one-half feet high.

Furniture making boomed during the early years of the colonial capital. Not until after 1725 did colonists begin importing chairs and other pieces of furniture from the northern colonies. Local chairmakers first used oak in the chairs they produced. While the chairs proved sturdy, they also proved heavy and difficult to maneuver. Constructed with solid square, panelled backs, these early creations were called "wainscot chairs." They also had solid wooden seats with heavy bracing underneath. Another early variety, also built of oak, featured elaborately carved designs and high, narrow backs with cane panels and cane seats. The rail-back chair, upholstered in leather or other fabric became fashionable just before the introduction of the light, comfortable Chippendale, Sheraton and Windsor chairs.

For some colonial Virginians, making a living was a sustained daily struggle. Unlike affluent landowners, small farmers planted some crops—like tobacco—that they could readily sell at market. Harvested staples like corn and wheat were carted off to a grist mill for grinding. The resulting sacks of wheat and flour became part of a home's stores for everyday cooking. Grist mills became a sign of healthy economic development for towns like Williamsburg and other nearby settlements. On March 2, 1693, the General Assembly passed legislation that sought to encourage the building of more wind-powered mills, as harnessing the prevailing breezes as a source of energy had proved efficient, especially where water power was not available.

Baked delights from Williamsburg ovens varied but generally reflected traditional English cooking. Some colonists liked bread made of wheat flour or corn meal. But use of wheat flour became the rule when it came to favorite dishes such as meat, chicken, fish, fruit or vegetable pies. Cooks mixed flour into paste, enclosed the main ingredient with paste crust and topping, and then baked the filled "pasties." As for other pastries, colonists enjoyed tarts in a variety of flavors as well as frosted layer cakes and mincemeat pies. Also popular were tasty gingerbread men and delicate lace cookies.

The butcher shop offered a variety of meats but pork and veal remained favorites in the capital. Mutton, chicken, turkey, duck, rabbit and even quail were also available, dressed and ready when colonists came shopping for dinner fare. Cattle, lean and tough like the deer, roamed the countryside, causing colonial consumers to seek more flavor and better texture in other meats, especially pork. Pigs often foraged in the forests, developing into leaner animals, but the quality of the meat surpassed beef. Colonists found that almost any complaint of taste and texture could be dismissed through the method of slow roasting the soft, pinkish pork over low hickory fires and aging the meat over a period of months. Pork enthusiasts took notice and the Virginia Ham became famous.

One of the many responsibilities of the colonial era wife was making the simple, homespun clothing worn by her working family. Spinning yarn, the first step in the process, meant drawing out fibers from a mass of raw material and twisting them in order to form an uninterrupted string of thread. Fibers came from cotton, wool or flax. Today, high-speed factory machines turn out thousands of yards of yarn per day. For colonial hand spinners, the process largely amounted to a slow and tedious chore.

Operating the loom—clothmaking's final phase—involved patience as well as creativity. The weaver's task included the interlacing of two sets of yarn, arranged on the loom at right angles. The concept of weaving is much like the process of basketmaking: Horizontal fibers are passed through sets of fibers arranged by length. The pair of top and bottom vertical sets are shifted to trap the horizontal threads which are passed back between them. Back and forth, the threads are woven, and the cloth is thus built thread by thread. The plain weave for homespun made strong cloth, fit for the times. In addition to clothing, colonists used home-made cloth for decorating their houses. These materials included bedspreads, bed "curtains" and window curtains, furniture upholstery and wall pictures. Colors came from dyes and embellishment of cloth into decorative patterns or images involved a long process of painstaking embroidery.

Gunsmiths ran lucrative businesses. After all, the capital existed as an oasis not far from dangerous frontiers—in all directions. To the colonists, carrying and using guns was a necessity for providing food and protection. Muzzle-loading English flintlocks (or Brown Bess) and pistols became standard arms of ordinary colonists and militia. Gunsmiths sold various types of firearms, including rifles brought to the colonies by Swiss and German settlers and the long fowling pieces. They also repaired the locks, stocks and barrels of a wide variety of firearms.

When Washington, Jefferson or Madison came to town, their first stop might have been at the Raleigh Tavern but, sooner or later, travelers found their way to the livery. Horses provided both a measure of personal freedom, as a means of transportation, and sport, through horse racing. The livery offered food and stabling for horses, harness repairs, rental carriages, and saddle horses as well as carriage and saddle repairs to the riding or horse-drawn public.

The colony's first printing establishment opened on Duke of Gloucester Street about 1730. William Parks owned the shop where he printed and sold a variety of publications. Early printers faced a lengthy process when producing books. Piece by piece, they set type in proper place and order. A hand-operated press turned out the pages, one at a time. But the demand for printed books steadily increased, as did the innovations to press and type that gradually made large jobs easier and faster. Parks founded the *Virginia Gazette*. The paper's first issue appeared in 1736. The Gazette has survived to this day. Later, Parks established a paper mill just outside the capital and advertised for "...all persons to save their old Linin Rags, for making paper." He concluded by saying, "...As this is the first Mill of the Kind, that ever was erected in this Colony, and has cost a very considerable Sum of Money."

Candlemakers gave light to Virginia's capital city. The Governor's Palace, the Capitol, and other major buildings featured massive chandeliers mounted with candles. Candles also illuminated interiors of the main rooms of the sometimes earthy, crowded rooms of the famous traverns. Most homes either did their own candle-making or bought what they needed at shops. Candle-wicks were either flax or cotton yarn. Colonists created dipped candles by cutting wicks to a desired length and stringing them from a frame placed over a large pot of melted wax. At intervals, wicks were dipped repeatedly into the hot wax until they were coated to an appropriate thickness. Finishing and smoothing completed the process.

Baskets are the most common product from the craft of weaving natural fibers together. At the basketmaker's shop in Williamsburg, work centered on constructing baskets that might have been used for marketing, storage or taking items from one place to another. Basketmakers also used their skills to weave cane seats for chairs. Materials for fiber weaving included twigs, roots, canes, and certain types of grasses. Colonial basketmakers learned some of their art from Indians of the region and from the African slaves brought to the colony. Women of the eastern American Indian tribes created baskets, mats, and belts from shredded bark, wood splints, and other native fibers.

America's first glassmaking operation began at Jamestown. A group of "Dutchmen and Poles," came to Virginia with Captain Christopher Newport in the fall of 1608. The men established a glass factory "in the woods, neare a myle from James Towne" in the spring of 1609. The winter of 1609 brought "The Starving Time," and no further mention of the European glassmakers appears in historical records. In 1621, an Englishman named William Norton and six Italian glassmakers arrived in Jamestown. They opened a glassworks but the Indian massacre of 1622 interrupted the effort and a storm destroyed the glasshouse. Excavations of glasshouse foundations revealed evidence that the early attempts at glassmaking produced little more than what might have been sample medicine bottles and other small vessels.

An apothecary served as the colonists' equivalent of today's pharmacist. Dr. Blair's apothecary shop could be found at the corner of Duke of Gloucester and Colonial Streets, offering a variety of elixers, ointments, and ingredients for remedies for a broad range of ailments. The April 4, 1766 edition of the *Virginia Gazette* reported arrival of a shipment of "Drugs and Medicines" from England. The assortment included: "...Florence and palm oil, mercurial and other ointments, plaisters, Bateman's drops, Anderson's pills, British oil, Squire's and Daffy's elixir, Godfrey's cordial, Stoughtone's bitters, Turlington's balsam of life..." At times, the apothecary was even called upon to perform minor surgeries.

Like their English forebears, Virginia colonists were garden enthusiasts and took pride in maintaining their own small plots. When Governor Francis Nicholson drew plans for Williamsburg as the new colonial capital, he specified each house should sit on a half-acre lot with room enough for a garden. Colonists planted herbs, vegetables and flowers. They harvested fruit from a variety of fruit trees. Hedges became popular, especially boxwood, as clipping did not become necessary for several years due to limited annual growth.

Dr. W.A.R. Goodwin, former Bruton Parish Church Rector and Head of the Department of Bibilical Literature and Religious Education at William and Mary had already plated the seeds for restoration when he convinced philanthropist John D. Rockefeller to fund the massive project. Together, they spearheaded the effort. Rockefeller provided financial and moral support while Rev. Goodwin built enthusiasm and acquired properties. Work began in 1927. In the years since, 609 modern buildings have been torn down or moved from the 3,000 acres purchased and more than 150 buildings restored or rebuilt. By the time of his death in 1960, Rockefeller had spent almost 68 million dollars. He also gave an endowment of 50 million dollars to the non-profit foundation that runs Colonial Williamsburg.

Restoration began with excavations on authenticated sites for houses, taverns, and shops. But the most dramatic discovery of the young project came in 1930 when archaeologists uncovered the foundations of the Governor's Palace. Excavations disclosed a configuration of foundation walls, fragments of walnut paneling in the main hall, fireplace tiles, stone steps, hinges, keys, and locks. The Palace had burned just after the Battle of Yorktown in 1781. The restoration project returned The Palace to its place as "a magnificent structure, built at public expense, finished and beautified with Gates, fine Gardens, Offices, Walks, a fine Canal, Orchards...by the ingenious Contrivance of the most accomplished Colonel (Royal Governor) Spotswood."

Bibliography

1. Abbot, William W. *A Virginia Chronology*. The Virginia 350th Anniversary Celebration Corporation. 1957.

2. Antiques Today Magazine, Editors. *Antiques and Williamsburg*. Hastings House. 1953.

3. Beverly, Robert . *The History and Present State of Virginia*. University of North Carolina Press. 1947.

4. Booth, Letha. *The Williamsburg Cookbook*. Colonial Williamsburg Foundation. 1975.

5. Bowie, Beverly M. "Williamsburg: Its College and Its Cinderella City," The National Geographic Magazine, Vol. CVI, No. 4, October, 1954.

6. Carrier, Lyman. *Agriculture in Virginia, 1607-1699*. The Virginia 350th Anniversary Celebration Corporation. 1957.

7. Colonial Williamsburg Foundation. *Williamsburg In Color*. Photos by Thomas L. Williams. 1954.

8. Craven, Wesley Frank. *The Virginia Company of London 1606-1624*. The Virginia 350th Anniversary Celebration Corporation. 1957.

9. Cumming, William P. *The Southeat and Early Maps*. Princeton University Press. 1958.

10. Davie, Emily. *Profile of America*. Thomas Y. Crowell Co. 1954.

11. Evans, Cerinda W. *Some Notes on Shipbuilding and Shipping in Colonial Virginia*. The Virginia 350th Anniversary Celebration Corporation. 1957.

12. Forman, Henry Chandler. *Virginia Architecture in the Seventeenth*. The Virginia 350th Anniversary Celebration Corporation. 1957.

13. Goldman, Eric F. " Firebrands of the Revolution," The National Geographic Magazine. Vol. 146, No. 1, July, 1974.

14. Goodwin, W. A. R. "The Restoration of Colonial Williamsburg," The National Geographic Magazine, Vol. LXXI, No. 4, April, 1937.

15. Hatch, Charles E. Jr. *The First Seventeen Years, Virginia 1607-1624*. The Virginia 350th Anniversary Celebration Corporation. 1957.

16. Herndon, Melvin . *Tobacco in Virginia, "The Sovereign Remedy."* The Virginia 350th Anniversary Celebration Corporation. 1957.

17. Hughes, Thomas P. *Medicine in Virginia, 1607-1609.* The Virginia 350th Anniversary Celebration Corporation. 1957.

18. Hume, Ivor Noel. *Here Lies Virginia.* Alfred A. Knopf. 1963.

19. Jester, Annie Lash. *Domestic Life in Virginia in the Seventeenth Century.* The Virginia 350th Anniversary Celebration. 1957.

20. Judge, Joseph. "Williamsburg, City for All Seasons," <u>The National Geographic Magazine</u>, Vol. 134, No. 6, December, 1968.

21. Kocher, A. Lawrence and Dearstyne, Howard *Colonial Williamsburg: Its Buildings and Gardens.* Colonial Williamsburg Foundation. 1949.

22. McCary, Ben C. *Indians in Virginia.* The Virginia 350th Anniversary Celebration Corporation. 1957.

23. Morton, Richard L. *Colonial Virginia, Vol. I., The Tidewater Period 1607-1610.* University of North Carolina Press. 1960.

24. Morton, Richard L. *Colonial Virginia Vol. II, Westward Expansion and Prelude to Revolution 1710-1763.* University of North Carolina Press. 1960.

25. Morton, Richard L. *Struggle Against Tyranny, and the Beginning of a New Era 1677-1699.* The Virginia 350th Anniversary Celebration Corporation. 1957.

26. Perry, Shaw and Hepburn, *The Restoration of Colonial Williamsburg, The Architectural Record.* Perry, Shaw and Hepburn, Architects. 1935.

27. Rutland, Robert Allen. *George Mason: Reluctant Statesman.* Colonial Williamsburg Foundation. 1961.

28. Stanard, Mary Newton. *Colonial Virginia: Its People and Customs.* Singing Tree Press. 1970.

29. Walklet, John J. and Ford, Thomas K. *A Window On Williamsburg,* Photos by Taylor Lewis Jr. Colonial Williamsburg Foundation. 1975.

30. Washburn, Wilcomb E.. *Virginia Under Charles I and Cromwell, 1625-1660.* The Virginia 350th Anniversary Celebration Corporation. 1957.

31. Wertenbaker, Thomas J. *Bacon's Rebellion.* The Virginia 350th Anniversary Celebration Corporation. 1957.

32. Wertenbaker, Thomas J. *The Government of Virginia in the Seventeenth Century.* The Virginia 350th Anniversary Celebration Corporation. 1957.

33. Wertenbaker, Thomas J. *The Shaping of Colonial Virginia.* Russell and Russell. 1958.

34. Wise, Felicity. *A Williamsburg Hornbook.* Stackpole Books. 1973.

35. Yetter, George Humphrey. *Williamsburg Before and After.* Colonial Williamsburg Foundation. 1988.